LIVING OFF THE GRID

A Step-By-Step Guide to a More Self-Sufficient, Self-Reliant, Sustainable Life

EMERSON WOODS

© 2016

TABLE OF CONTENTS

Emerson Woods Copyright © 2016

INTRODUCTION

Living off the grid means living a self-sufficient life on infrastructure and a system that are designed to function properly without support from the power grid or public utilities. This means that off the grid homes are instead powered by a standalone power system (or in the case of off the grid communities, the homes can either be powered standalone or by a collective power system used by the entire community).

People live off the grid mainly for one of two reasons: 1. They may live in an area that has insufficient access to power and electricity, such as a more distant location, or 2. They may voluntarily choose to live off the grid regardless of whether or not they live close to electrical access.

Why would someone choose to voluntarily live off the grid? For one thing, no longer being reliant on a utility company for your power and water is a huge plus. If the power grid ever goes down due to a natural disaster or an EMP attack, your home can still be running! It's this kind of self-sufficiency that attracts so many people to off the grid living in the first place.

The additional benefits to living off the grid is that it's greener for the environment, gives you more financial freedom, and can enable you to feel less stress.

Contrary to what people think, you don't have to live remotely or in a rural area to live off the grid. There are people who live in urban or suburban environments who supply themselves with their own power as well. It's something that anybody can do.

According to *USA Today*, there are currently an estimated 200,000 homes that are off the grid and supplying themselves with their own power. There are an additional 30,000 homes that live partially off the grid, meaning they are still technically connected to the power grid. These homes rely on some self-sustainable power such as wind energy or solar power. Most of these partial off the grid homes are located in more urban or suburban areas.

The primary goal of this e-book is to give you an introduction to the basics of off the grid living and what you can expect from it. We're going to cover lifestyle changes you have to make, how to be self-sufficient on your own water, the pros and cons of solar vs. wind power, how to find the right land for living off the grid, how to grow or raise your own food, off the grid communities, and then any final tips we haven't covered yet.

Let's get started!

CHAPTER 1: LIFESTYLE CHANGES

The biggest change that comes with living off the grid is going to be the lifestyle changes that you must make. We're not going to lie: living off the grid is a ton of work! There's far more work to be put in living off the grid than there is living on it. Some people who live off the grid embrace this challenge while others do not anticipate it, so it's important that you are at least aware of them.

Living off the grid isn't for people who can't physically handle a few chores (such as chopping firewood), for people who want instant gratification or who don't want to be involved in their home, and people who aren't ready to make some necessary sacrifices. Most would also argue that the financial, environmental, and stress-free benefits of off the grid living far outweigh its challenges.

Regardless of whether you consider these to be positives or negatives, here are some of the certain lifestyle changes you will have to make if you choose to live off the grid:

Off the Grid Living Requires Responsibility

Living off the grid is not uncomfortable. Those who believe that living off the grid means living in a cold, damp, and dark house are incredibly mistaken. In living off the grid your home will be more responsibly heated, lit, and insulated.

The idea that off the grid living is uncomfortable is a massive misconception because it's actually more comfortable, but notice the word that we used: responsibility. There's a lot of responsibility that goes into making your off the grid home more comfortable than a normal home.

Later on in this book, we will explore many ways for how you can become self-sufficient on your off the grid home in regards to food, water, power, and so on. All of these techniques involve responsibility, but at the same time, it's always convenient when your food is home grown in your backyard and your solar energy is free and powered by the sun, right? It turns out that responsibility and convenience go hand in hand.

Off the Grid Living Means You Must Learn and Apply New Skills

A major lifestyle change of living off the grid is having to learn new skills and then apply those new skills on a daily basis. In the world that we live in now, whenever we need something, all that we really have to do is buy it. Or if we require the services of a professional, we just make a phone call.

Off the grid living works differently because it pushes you to provide yourself with your own necessities and to fix anything that gets broken. In generating your own power, for example, you have to learn how to maintain your power system and monitor your consumption. You apply the skills that you learn daily in order to keep your power system up and running. The same applies to food, water, and other things as well.

Off The Grid Living Forces You to Live With, Not In, a Place

This is perhaps the biggest lifestyle change of all because fundamentally, with an off the grid home you are not living in a place, but rather with nature. You'll be spending a lot more time outside at your location, and as a result you'll be paying significantly more attention to the natural world around you because it is providing you with everything that you need.

Nature provides you with the food that you grow, the water that you drink, and the power that gives warmth to your home. When you live off the grid, you are living with whatever the sky and the land are providing you, how and when they provide it to you, and how you can preserve or monitor your consumption of those provisions.

Hopefully all three of these major lifestyle changes are positives for you! Most people who turn to off the grid living fully embrace the concept of living more responsibly, learning and applying new skills, and working with nature. It can lead to a more fulfilling life that's impossible to discover with your current way of living.

CHAPTER 2: WATER

Our next few chapters are going to dive into how to live off the grid. Our first topic is being self-sustainable on water.

Water is something that we all need to survive. It's refreshing and it gives us new life and energy when we have gone long without it. But the real beauty of it is how available it is. Think about it. Water is literally everywhere!

It's in the sky in the form of rain, on the ground in the form of rivers and lakes, and under the ground as well. You can tap into any one of these sources, or all three of them, to become self-sustainable on water. In addition, it's estimated that 17 million (or 15% of all) homes in the U.S.A are already self-sustainable on water according to the EPA, so there is little reason to think why you can't do the same as well.

Private Wells

The vast majority of those 17 million homes get their water from underground sources via private wells. The principle of a private well is very simple. You dig or drill a hole deep into the ground and then install a pump to draw out the water.

Well, if it were only that simple. Private wells are effective and a great way to be self-sustainable on water because restrictions on water in the event of a drought won't apply to you, but they are also expensive to install and there are a lot of regulations that you have to navigate as well. The cost of a private well varies anywhere from three to fifteen thousand dollars; the cost is dependent on how far down you need to go. The deeper down you go, the cleaner the water will be, so plan on spending closer to fifteen thousand than three thousand if you want higher quality water.

That doesn't include the cost of hiring a licensed well driller to dig and install it for you as well. You will want to go with a licensed well driller as they are already fully aware of the rules and regulations on the books and will also make sure that no harmful contaminants leak into your well.

Private wells are a popular and very effective means to be reliant on your own water; they just can be a hassle and are expensive to install.

Water Cisterns

An alternative to a water pump is to harvest your own water via a water cistern. A cistern is a very large tank that holds water and is made out of steel, fiberglass, or concrete. It can be set up either above ground or underground.

How a cistern works is that rainwater will channel through the cistern and then be pumped back into your house as you need it. If your cistern is an above the ground model, you can use the water weight as pressure when getting it into your home. In contrast to this, water cisterns that are below ground will require a pump in order to get the water to you (very similar to a private well).

The disadvantage to water cisterns is obvious: no rain, no water! This is why you should only install a water cistern if you live in an area that gets plenty of rain such as the Pacific Northwest. If you live in an area that gets plenty of rain, a water cistern will be a cheaper option than a private well. Otherwise, you should go with a well.

Septic System

While we are talking about water, we should also talk about installing a septic system. You can't go truly off the grid without installing your own septic system.

What an off the grid septic system will comprise of is a large sized, metal tank that collects and then releases your wastewater. Bacteria present inside of the tank will break down the waste and separate it into a top, middle, and bottom layer.

The liquid in the tank then flows out into buried pipes that take the liquid over a distance before releasing it into a drain field. Soil will act as a filter to keep the bacteria buried beneath the ground and absorbed as nutrients. You should have your tank emptied and serviced at least once a year.

CHAPTER 3: SOLAR VS. WIND POWER

Our next chapter is going to talk about how you can power your off the grid home with renewable energy. By way and large, the two most popular renewable energy options for powering off the grid houses are solar and wind power. We're going to discuss the pros and cons of each in this chapter.

But before we do, what's imperative for you to know is that you must rid yourself of being dependent on a power company's electricity to go off the grid. So regardless of whether you go with wind or solar power, just know that you're definitely on the right course by choosing either of them. Neither solar power or wind power is a new concept, but they both definitely have been proven to work. It ultimately is based on your personal preference and the circumstances of your land.

Solar Power

Many off the grid homes make use of PV (photovoltaic) solar panels that are located on the roof of the house or by the house. Each panel is made up of silicon semiconductors in its cells. Whenever the light of the sun hits the panel, the semiconductors collect the energy and this allows electrons to flow freely and form an electric field in one direction. This electric field is called an electrical direct current.

The electrical direct current then passes through an inverter that converts it into the alternative current power your home will use.

When one thinks of off the grid power systems, solar panels are probably what come to mind first. It can provide plenty of electrical power as long as you get enough exposure to the sun in your area. Solar panels also require little maintenance and have few moving parts.

But there's an inevitable downside to everything, and in the case of solar power, it's the cost. Solar power is not the most cost-effective way to power an entire home, and when you combine that with the fact that it only works when the sun is shining, you can start to see how it is not a definitive solution to powering an off the grid home.

Wind Power

Wind power is the same way. It's a viable solution for powering a home, but it also has its pros and cons and isn't a definitive solution.

Wind power is run by wind turbines that look like airplane propellers. They sit atop thin towers that can measure anywhere from fifty to one hundred and twenty feet high. Whenever the wind blows, the blades will move and spin a shaft leading from the rotor to the generator.

The generator will then take the energy that has been produced from the turbine's rotation and converts it into electricity. Just like how solar panels work, an inverter is also installed to convert the electricity into AC power that you can use.

The biggest advantage to wind power over solar power, or any other kind of power for that manner, is that it is cheaper and cleaner. The average cost per kilowatt per hour for wind power is only three cents. Contrast this with the ten cents it costs for making use of coal burning electricity. Combine this, then, with the fact that wind power produces no greenhouse emissions and it's easy to see why many people who live off the grid have turned to wind power.

But there's an obvious downside to wind power as well. Just like how solar panels require enough sunlight, wind turbines require enough wind. No electricity is generated if the turbine stays still.

The size of the turbine also matters. The bigger the turbine, the more electricity it produces. A turbine rotor that measures four feet in diameter will produce about four hundred watts - enough to power a few appliances. A seven foot turbine will produce nine hundred watts, and a twenty-three foot turbine (which is out of the budget of many people who live off the grid) produces ten thousand watts and must sit on a pole that is at least one hundred feet tall. Obviously, a turbine of this size is not going to work if you live on a smaller plot of land or in a suburban/urbanized area.

Another downside that wind turbines have vs. solar panels is they typically require more maintenance. With solar panels, you have few moving parts so maintenance is kept to a minimum. It's not the same story with wind turbines. Since more parts are moving, more parts have the possibility of failure.

Hybrid System

A more reliable option to power your off the grid home is to install a hybrid system, which combines solar power and wind power so you receive the best of both worlds. If sunlight fails, at least you'll still have the wind, and vice versa.

But not even a hybrid system is without its downsides, and in this case it's the fact that creating a hybrid system means your electricity will be stored by a utility company. Fortunately, forty states currently have laws that permit you to sell your electricity back to the company for some extra cash on the side if what you produce exceeds your consumption. At the same time, you may not like the fact that you're still technically connected to a power company. For this reason, some people consider off the grid homes that use hybrid systems to not be truly off the grid.

CHAPTER 4: LAND

Do you know how to find the right land for your off the grid home? The good news is that as long as you do, finding a suitable plot of land should be one of the easiest steps towards transitioning to an off the grid home.

This chapter is going to talk about four very important factors that you must absolutely consider when purchasing new land for your off the grid home so that you know exactly what you need:

Practicality

This one is easily the most important factor of all. You have to purchase land that naturally lends itself to an off the grid house. This means that your land needs to support self-sustainable living and renewable energy. Therefore, if your home is in the middle of a grove of trees, it's certainly going to receive a diminished amount of wind for turbines and possibly a lesser amount of sun for solar power and may not be the greatest option. Or if you live on land that is very uneven, it could mean that installing your own sewage system of pipes will be a hassle. These are the kinds of things that you will need to keep in mind.

Take note that practicality means more than just the land itself. It also means being on land where the legalities of city ordinances, building codes, and restrictions are all in order and where the price is right for you. Even if you find the perfect piece of property, it would still be unwise to spend money that you don't have on it if it's too expensive.

Location

The physical location of your home is also very important. What we mean by this is its proximity to urban areas. Many off the grid homes are built in rural locations out in the countryside, but many others are constructed in suburban and urban locations as well. If you need to live near town for cost or work-related reasons, you can still live off the grid. In short, you should live in a location that is best for your needs.

As long as the land that you choose is practical, living off the grid either in the country or near a city is possible. Some people who live off the grid prefer to live in the countryside away from town in order to be 'truly' off the grid, while others prefer to live near town if their work requires them to do so.

Climate

The type of climate that you choose will ultimately depend on the type of power that you choose to generate, or vice versa. Solar and wind power, as we have already gone over, are by far your two best options. Therefore, your climate will need plenty of sun and/or wind, so a cold or wet climate may not be the best idea for an off the grid location.

Water

Water is absolutely a factor to consider all on its own. We can't live without it and it would be very unwise to select an off the grid location where you have to travel for miles before you find it. Your land needs to have a natural source of clean water either on it or nearby if you want to be truly self-sustainable. Relying on water from the grocery store or having to haul containers of it in the back of your truck for miles back to your house is simply not self-sustainable living.

Examples of reliable natural water sources include wells, lakes, streams, rivers, and natural springs. Rainwater is also a natural source of water, but you can't always count on it to rain, which is why additionally having one of the other options we listed a very good idea. Store your water in a clean storage tank that's kept in a cool and dark location, keep track of when it was accumulated, and have a reliable filter system on standby.

CHAPTER 5: FOOD

Our next chapter is going to discuss how you can become self-sustainable on food. Being self-sustainable on food means that you have to grow it or raise it on your own. Just like how solar and wind power are best for generating your house with power, and how water cisterns and private wells are the best options for producing self-sustainable water, gardening and livestock are your two best options for being self-reliant on food.

Gardening

We'll start with gardening. Gardening is not only an important homesteading skill, it's an important life skill. Once you've got the basics of gardening down, you'll find that it's very helpful for providing yourself and your family with valuable food and medicine. Gardening is also a continual learning process, so you'll hone your skills each season.

Most homesteaders garden both indoors and outdoors. A core principle of gardening, especially in the planning stage, is maximizing space. You have to decide what you want to grow and what grows together well (and not well), but you need to make sure that you grow enough of a crop so that you can be truly self-reliant on the food in your garden.

When drawing your blue print for the garden, make sure that plants that grow well together (such as carrots and tomatoes) are grown next to one another so that as little space as possible is wasted.

When selecting the location for your garden, the amount of natural sunlight it receives (in the case of outdoor gardens at least, with indoor gardens you can use UV rays) is the most important factor. Some crops such as beans, cabbage, corn, eggplants, tomatoes, peppers, and all kinds of melons require at least six hours of sunlight a day and can only be grown in a spot with full sun. Lettuce, spinach, kale, peas, carrots, beets, and potatoes require four hours of sunlight per day, and can get by in a location that receives only partial sunlight.

At this point you have decided what kinds of plants you will be gardening and where you will be gardening them. Now it's time to build your beds. Your beds will have to be designed so that they can be reached from all sides. This is why many garden beds you see are very long and narrow, so that you can easily walk around them and attend every square inch of the soil inside of it. A length of nine feet and a width of three feet will accomplish this.

As far as the number of beds are concerned, bear in mind that you will need to rotate your crops, so building beds in multiples of four is a good rule of thumb to follow.

Once your gardening beds have been built, it's time to prepare your soil. Fill up the beds until the soil has reached a depth of anywhere from twelve to eighteen inches, and then even them out with a rake or shovel. Purchase a soil test kit to test out your soil; the test kit tells you how you need to fertilize your soil and what kind of organic matter or compost to add. If your soil doesn't have good drainage, sand will be a welcome addition.

Compost is your best option for adding organic materials to your garden. Not only is it effective, but it's free if you make it yourself: just add vegetable matter from your kitchen into your compost pile. Avoid animal matter.

Your garden requires that you tend to it on a daily basis once your crops have been planted. Not only do you need to tend to your garden by watering it and check up on how well your plants are growing, but also to keep pests out of the way in the form of slugs, weeds, and deer. Construct a fence around your garden to keep the deer away and spray it with insecticide to keep slugs and insects away too. As for the weeds, you can pull and then add them to your compost material.

We can't go into how to raise and care for your actual herbs and crops just because there are so many different kinds out there and each of them have their own unique requirements. However, you now have a good idea of how to set up your garden regardless of what crop(s) you decide to go with.

What we can tell you is that when you water your garden, it should be done at least twice each week for a thirty minute period at the minimum; exceptions apply to hotter and drier climates where you'll need to water more often, or if a plant has a specific need. Water the plants either early in the morning or later in evening.

Livestock

We're now going to discuss raising livestock. Most people who are planning on living off the grid in a suburban location or anywhere close to a town or city may think that gardening is their only choice for being self-reliant on food. But this could not be any further from the truth.

Even if you live in a suburban or urban environment, you can still provide you and your family with fresh meat and eggs. Let's run down the list of what kind of livestock are available for you to raise:

The first livestock we will talk about are chickens because they are arguably the easiest to raise and keep. Plus, it's legal to raise chickens in several areas near towns as well (check up on your local laws). Chicken hens will provide you and your family with a reasonable amount of daily eggs, while you can grow your flock with the addition of a rooster. Each chicken requires three square feet of space in a nesting box.

Rabbits are also very easy to take care of because they take up very little space and don't require a lot to eat. They also provide great compost and fertilizer for your garden and with two pairs of healthy breeding rabbits in your coop, in a matter of weeks you'll be putting rabbit meat on the dining room table several times a week. The only reason why we rank rabbits below chickens is because they are very messy, and you'll need to spend a lot of time cleaning up their pen.

Raising ducks is very similar to raising chickens. They are very quiet and they produce fertilized eggs as well. The only downside to ducks is that they require more space than chickens or rabbits.

Each duck will require at least four or five square feet of space in their coop, and that's not counting the additional amount of space that they need to run around in.

When you can't raise chickens, you can always raise quail. What we mean by this is that in areas where it's illegal to raise chickens, it usually is legal to raise quail because they are smaller. They also require less food and space, and are very quiet birds as well. Quail also grow quickly and will begin laying eggs from the age of six weeks on. The downside to Quail is that they produce smaller eggs and don't have much meat on themselves either.

Perhaps the most multipurpose domesticated animal that you can raise as livestock is sheep. They produce wool, milk, and meat. Yes, milking them can be a hassle as they can get very nervous and kick at you during the milking process, but the trade off is that the milk is very high quality. Each sheep will require at least sixteen square feet of living space. The downside to sheep is that they are not very friendly, so be prepared to deal with them. An alternative to sheep would be goats, but goats are also less multipurpose than sheep are.

Finally, cows are another excellent livestock option. They are a great animal to raise even if you don't have a sprawling ranch for a herd to live on; just having two or three cows in a large fenced area will suffice for off the grid purposes. Like sheep, cows are also multipurpose and provide you with meat, dairy, and leather. The most significant downside to them is that they require the most space out of all of the animals on this list, so if you live on a smaller plot of land near a town, they are simply not an option.

CHAPTER 6: COMMUNITY

Something to consider when preparing to go off the grid is whether or not you will live by yourself or in an off grid community. The mere concept of off the grid living has become so popular at this point that there's entire real estate developments dedicated just to it. Off the grid communities are also known as self-sustainable communities or off the grid colonies.

An immediate benefit to living in an off the grid community is that it practically solves the issue of finding a suitable plot of land for your house as long as you don't mind being lumped closely to other people.

Off the grid communities began to take form in America in the late 1960s and early 1970s. While there are still plenty of people today who prefer to live an off the grid lifestyle in solitude at a private location, there are definitely plenty of others who have embraced the idea of a sustainable community. Almost all off the grid communities rely on solar power and will have a natural water source nearby.

Earlier in this book we noted a *USA Today* statistic that estimated the minimum number of American homes to be completely off the grid at 180,000 and rising. A majority of those homes are individual homes outside of a community, but an increasing number of them are in one.

If you're on the fence about whether or not an off the grid community is right for you, we've outlined and discussed some major factors to consider to aid in your decision making process:

Shelter

Next to a water source, having an adequate shelter is probably the most important factor of living off the grid. The homes at an off the grid community will have to be well-built and insulated if you are considering one. You should reject a community where the homes are poorly constructed or have been improperly maintained. Alternatively, you can always build your own house on the community too so long as they allow and if so, that it meets their regulations.

Privacy

If you do end up choosing to move to an off the grid community, you will have to decide whether or not you will be living in your own house or if you will be sharing the house with another family or individual.

It's fully understandable if you need your privacy and don't want your family to be bunking in next to another; in fact, the strong majority of people probably fall into this camp.

If you do choose to live in your own home, the question that pops up next is how close the houses are to one another. Are the homes and the main lodge area more spread out so that each has its own fair amount of acreage, or are the homes situated more closely together like in a traditional neighborhood? Additionally, are the homes and properties separated from one another by things such as trees or a fence that provide at least privacy?

Privacy is a very important issue and it's critical that everyone respect one another's boundaries. If an off grid community you find has homes that are too close to one another or that aren't separated by trees, all you have to do is say 'no.'

What Can You Contribute?

Everyone who lives in an off grid community will be bringing to the table their own knowledge and skills that they can contribute. Everyone also has the ability to reach out to others and to share their knowledge with them. This sharing of knowledge is ultimately what grows the community as a whole.

Obviously some people may not be able to contribute as much to the community as other people can. Some individuals may have health issues that mean they can't work in hard labor, for example. But at the end of the day, everyone is able to contribute at least something even if some do more than others.

When considering an off the grid community, you have to think about what you can contribute as a part of it, and what you are willing and not willing to contribute. If you decide are unable to contribute as much as other people in the community can, then it may not be right for you.

How Will the Community Produce Water and Food?

A community that is truly self-sustaining has to produce enough food and water on its own to feed everybody. Water should be a given without second thought. There has to be a clean and natural water source to provide people with enough water for drinking, sanitation, and cooking purposes. Many books and online articles have been written on this subject alone. Ultimately, water will be produced by a natural source just like the one you would use in an individual off the grid home such as a well, lake, river, or spring, but there has to be enough water to sustain everybody.

Ensuring that everything is kept sanitary and clean is also vitally important and it's yet another reason why a clean water source is so important. The health of the members of the community is at stake if it is not kept clean. If an off the grid community you visit seems to have fallen behind in the sanitation department, you would be wise to avoid it. We'll touch more on this in a little bit.

As for food, the crops will most likely be grown in a large community garden. This garden will usually be between ten to twenty acres and be entirely dedicated to growing crops and herbs, raising the livestock, and perhaps even having a pond of fish. To give you an idea of how much food an off the grid community needs, American adults on average consume one ton of food individually per year. Then multiply this by the number of people in your community and you'll arrive at the number for how much food the community needs to sustain itself adequately.

When visiting an off the grid community to see if it works for you, ask about where and how food is grown. There are many special gardening techniques that allow as much crops to be grown as possible in as little of a surface area that there is. If a community uses this principle over a large field of ten acres or more, then they should be on the right track in the food department.

How Are Disagreements Handled in the Community?

This is a factor that many people who move into off grid communities didn't really take into consideration before they moved into one, only to possibly find out later that no real rules were in place. It's perfectly reasonable to assume that a community can't prepare or plan for every single kind of a disagreement that can happen, but it should still have a set of fair and basic rules that everyone knows about and agrees to before moving in.

Everyone's voice in the community should absolutely be heard equally and every individual should have an equal vote when holding elections or deciding community policy. Avoid communities where it appears that the rules have purposefully given certain people more power or influence than others rather than treating everybody equally. Most communities will likely have a board of some sort where a small group of people have been elected to handle the community's finances, and this is absolutely fine. You just don't want to live in a community where the 'governing authority' shuts out other people's opinions or doesn't give everyone an equal say.

It is inevitable as a pure result of human nature that disputes will occur in any community. Any successful community should have a list of basic rules already set up that are designed to keep the peace, and an off grid community is certainly no exception.

How is Waste Handled in the Community?

We've touched on cleanliness and sanitation already in this chapter. We'll discuss it in greater depth here. Plain and simple, if an off grid community lacks proper sanitation it is at large risk of diseases spreading. This is one reason why a good and clean water source is so vital.

There also needs to be a septic system installed in the community. However, there are a variety of different ways that septic systems are handled in off grid communities as well. Some communities have each house or cabin installed with a septic system already, while others have a central bathroom area that will empty out into a community septic system. Other communities may have a combination of the two.

Ultimately what matters more than the septic system is that everything is kept clean and sanitary, but if an off grid community you visit has no septic system in place or a poor one, avoid that community at all costs.

Is There a Community Center?

It's generally a good idea for an off grid community to have some sort of a community center. The reason for this is because it's a location where the community members can socialize, meet new members, and hold parties and events. However, it's not a must have in a community so it ultimately boils down to your preference.

Those are the factors that you should take into the strongest consideration when thinking about an off grid community. A strong majority of people who live off the grid live individually because they enjoy the solitude and privacy; it's perfectly understandable why.

But if you do choose to live in an off grid community rather than your own private house, the community at the bare minimum must have adequate cabins or homes, a natural and clean water source, enough food growing or being raised to feed and sustain everyone continuously, a system on how to handle disagreements and to ensure that everyone is treated equally with an equal vote, and a reliable septic system that keeps the community as sanitary as possible.

Chapter 7: Final Tips

This chapter is going to cover a series of tips that we haven't covered yet, but that will also make your off the grid lifestyle and the process of transitioning to it much smoother.

Tip #1: Involve Your Entire Family

Children are much more industrious and smart than adults commonly give them credit for, and that includes small children. Children will view changing to an off the grid lifestyle as an adventure and will likely be more than willing to help out however they can. Young children in particular will delight in feeding your rabbits or chickens, for example. Keep all of the hard work for yourself, obviously, but find ways to involve your children in the process as well by giving them tasks that they can handle and enjoy responsibly.

Tip #2: Have a Goal

Living off the grid is the exact opposite of laziness. The vast majority of those who live off the grid are very industrious people with a clear goal in mind. They work very hard to do it for themselves by setting things at their own tastes. Having a clear goal in your mind is what it will take to focus on what's important in living off the grid and to remember that you're no longer being dictated by somebody else.

Tip #3: Have a Backup Power System

Spending the money on a reliable biodiesel or good gas generator will sooner or later prove to be a good investment. Yes, either wind turbines and solar panels should serve as your primary power system. At the same time, it's possible that either of those systems could fail. While in the process of repairing a broken panel or turbine, a generator can supply you with power. Set aside gasoline that is dedicated just for your generator and is kept separate from the gas you have stored away for vehicles. Ideally, you should have enough gasoline set aside for your generator for it to run for three days at the minimum; some say you should even have enough for a full week.

Tip #4: Get into the Mode of Money Saving

There are a host of different ways that you can reduce how much money you spend; the saved money can then be re-invested into things such as savings or paying for your off the grid lifestyle.

A few ideas for how you can reduce your expenses include eliminating club memberships, canceling credit cards that you don't use, opting out of gym memberships, trading in your cars for older but reliable models for a lower monthly payment, eating out less often, using coupons at the grocery store, and so on. An entire book could be written on each expense reduction you could make and how to make it.

Admittedly, reducing expenses can be a hard thing to do for some people. There's no shame if you struggle with the idea of reducing some of your current expenses as a result of the sacrifices that you'll have to make. However, having too many possessions can actually get in your way if you want to downsize in your off the grid home. Focus on your essentials and what you need. It's still fine to buy things that you want, as you should spend at least a little bit of your money on 'fun things,' but you can't let that take a sizable chunk out of your paycheck.

Tip #5: Learn New Survival Skills

We've touched on this one in this book already and there's no doubt that you'll be learning survival skills in the process of your off the grid lifestyle. But it certainly doesn't hurt to pick up on a few critical wilderness survival skills between now and moving into your off the grid home. You can do this by camping out in the wild or taking a wilderness survival course. This can give you a head start on your off the grid living.

There are certain survival skills we very much recommend you learn before living off the grid. The first is to know how to use some basic weapons and tools. The second is to learn about food preservation techniques and how to cure meat so you can use it for later. All of these skills will come in handy and give you less road bumps when you actually start to garden and raise your own livestock.

Tip #6: Make Some Dietary Changes

A large majority of people who go off the grid make a goal of living a healthier lifestyle, and there's a good chance that you've thought about this yourself. Part of living a healthier lifestyle is to eat a natural diet rather than processed foods. Try including more and more natural foods in your diet right now while in the process of transitioning from your current home to your off grid one. When living on your homestead fully self-sufficient, most of your diet is going to consists of grains, fruits, vegetables, and meat.

Tip #7: Patience

An off the grid house is going to be a major lifestyle change for you, and the process of transitioning to it from where you are now is going to be a project. You can't expect to just be moved in and settled in a month. You have to build your own renewable energy system, possibly build your own house, install your own septic system, and so on. These kinds of things take time, and while it's understandable that you are excited to begin your new lifestyle, having patience will yield you the best rewards.

Tip #8: Make Time for Outdoor Hobbies

While you'll have to work hard living a self-sufficient life, you should still include other fun outdoor activities and hobbies in order to balance the work out. An outdoor hobby to spend time on can be anything you desire from hiking, camping, fishing, working in the garden, bird watching, or even just sitting in a lawn chair.

Tip #9: Don't Think You Have to Live as a Recluse

Getting away from the power grid and the hustle of city life does not mean that you will be cutting off ties. You can still keep your connections to friends and family members via the internet, phones, and by visiting. You may find that your social life is actually improved as you have fun experiences and stories to share with others. Needless to say, the perception that off the grid living means living alone out in a remote house with little to no contact with the outside world is a drastically misinformed viewpoint of what off the grid living truly is.

Tip #10: Keep Learning!

You can never learn too much about off the grid living and you'll very likely learn something new every day. Treat your education of survival and self-sufficient living as a lifelong process and you are bound to be happy and successful in your off the grid house.

In due course, you'll find that deciding to live off the grid may have been the best decision you ever made.

CONCLUSION

Congratulations on reading this e-book! You have just been given a comprehensive overview of what off the grid living is and what you can expect to do in order to live off the grid.

In a world where nearly everybody is connected to the power grid for electricity and water, and on grocery stores for food, it can give you a whole new feeling of confidence and security to be totally self-sufficient in all of those things. If anything ever happens to the grid and people are scrambling for water, food, and power, you won't be. This alone is one of the greatest benefits for both families and individuals who live off the grid. No longer are you or your family dependent on supermarkets, city water, sewage systems, or an electrical company.

Obviously this isn't anywhere close to the total amount of information that you can learn in regards to off the grid living, but we hope that you now have a much clearer picture of how you and your family can live off the grid and see why so many other people have chosen to do so. You can refer back to this e-book at any time for information as you embark on your off grid lifestyle.

Good luck!

REVIEW

Thanks again for purchasing and reading *this book*.

As a self-published author, I love to know what the reader thinks. ☺ If you have a moment, please leave a review for my book on Amazon.

54294577R00027

Made in the USA
Charleston, SC
30 March 2016